This Business of Becoming Mad

This Business of Becoming Mad

K. Rose Quayle

Copyright © 2021 K. Rose Quayle

The moral right of this author has been asserted.

All rights reserved.

No part of this publication may be reproduced, stored in a retrieval system, or transmitted, in any form or by any means, without the prior permission in writing of the publisher, nor be otherwise circulated in any form of binding or cover other than that in which it is published and without a similar condition being imposed on the subsequent purchaser.

Cover art Copyright © 2021 K. Rose Quayle

Book design and production by K. Rose Quayle

Published by K. Rose Quayle

Pittsburgh, PA, United States of America

Photos by K. Rose Quayle, author photo by D. Chalich

For Tim.

I miss you.

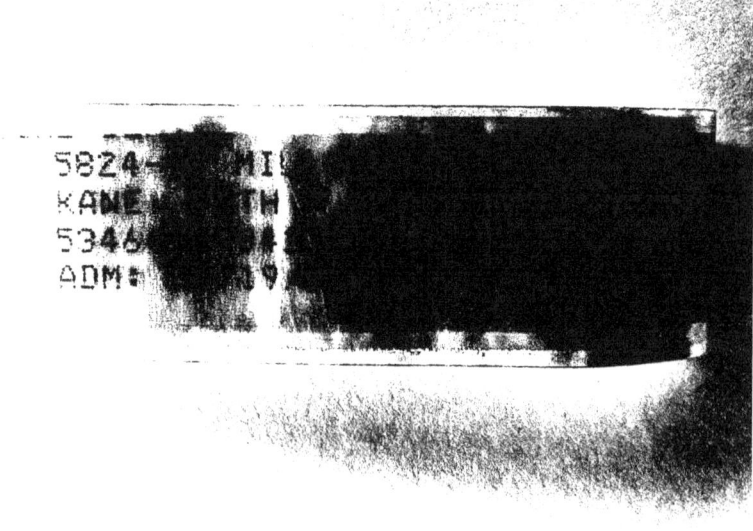

5824

I wake,

and where They are glad to see another day,

I'm crestfallen that I'm still here.

These hanging bags, my life's safeguard

filling me with the breath I do not crave.

But as soon as I can speak,

They fold me up and send me, tagged

to *that* place upon *that* hill.

I'm taken to the white room

screams dribble through the walls.

They take my shoes and garments,

give me my number and my gown

consign to me new aliases

then sit me down to this wretched work,

this business of becoming mad.

Are We Not Broken?

Are we not, are we not broken?
Did G-d forget to stitch us up?
A heart of tinfoil, a mind misplaced
excelsior spoiled, leaking about the joints
a button eye cracked, a shank removed
are we not, are we not broken?

I watch through the window to the ward next over
nurses are scurrying, doctors ordering
orderlies fetching
We'll stitch your arm, we'll set your leg
we'll put your sugar to right
and then you'll be cured and off you go
back to sleep in your own bed.

But there is no *cure* for an addled brain
in *these* halls, none expected to come
this word, foreign and cottony in the mouth
lunacy holds one in its own leg-irons
no cards, no flowers, no wishes well.
And when they turn us out again
no-one wants us home.

But are we not, are we not broken?

Did G-d forget to stuff in our souls as with other folk?

So there is no way to mend us?

No stitches, casts or pins

to keep manias inside us

to keep demons sliding out.

Bells give wings to angels

flowers give love to the sick

but rope-bruises give us our definition,

diagnosed, packaged and branded

a hemstitch frayed and sagging.

Are we not, are we not broken?

Zoo Walks

We love to look down this particular hill to the bus stop

and hope they're looking up at us

feeling bad that someone locked us up

and isn't bothered to visit.

They say we're

loud and impertinent

and *absolutely inappropriate*

prodigious and childlike

magnificent and insane

murderous and angelic

never right and never wrong

with a sixth sense

a common sense

no sense

a genius mind

a beautiful mind

a broken mind

Little animals taking zoo walks

scaring all the tamed people

til they lock us up again.

Kicking the world about like a soccer ball

And clutching it like a doll;

Window-shopping for someone else's mind.

Damned to be forever-children but

Clever enough to know adults only know better ways to lie.

We'll stay here then in the castle

in our cages, looking down the hill.

We Don't Smile

We don't smile.

Lest a shine of depravity would gleam on our faces,

lest a murderous click ring out from our teeth.

We rock in the halls, back and forth to that

lullaby of dementia,

twirling our bracelets, we don't give up

any evidence.

We don't smile.

We don't smile.

They have a term for it- *flat effect.*

We have a term too- *defiance.*

They will hurt us to help us

we will refuse and lose

it's all right, this is how we fight

we are our own allies.

We don't smile.

We don't smile.

They take us out to walk in the streets

they tell us *don't try to run.*

Like microchipped dogs,

we are always aware of our of identities.

Craziness might hide underneath our spots

but someone always knows it's there.

We don't smile.

We don't smile.

On the television: a stream of scenes

chopped and scattered like puzzle blocks

watching the flow of life pass by

deaths, births, commercials

standing this side of the glass watching

our old world leave us behind.

We don't smile.

We don't smile.

We hear them speak our words without permission

trigger, anxiety, addiction

but wear not the scars to earn them.

We hear them talk of *awareness*

without being aware they steal from us.

We're no longer sure who They are and who They aren't,

yet They still wonder why-

we don't smile?

There was no Body for the Elegy

Bone shadows stretch across the hall.
We've been keeping vigil for hours, knowing
there will be no body for the elegy.
The essence of one woman's life
has been wiped clean from her room
as if she'd never existed on the sheets carrying her stain.
as if she'd never existed in the world which printed it there.

There wasn't enough staff to check on her.
There wasn't enough funding to go round.
Our sister was fallen and taken away from our Ward.
We are tenacious. We do not accept defeat.
We do not know if death has yet come in our midst
so we watch for the sickle.
For we cannot accept!
She was supposed to be safe from herself-
Who shall it be next?

A solitary nurse stripped her name from the door-
and a new sister came
for no-one's memory is allowed to stay
in these halls of transience
and we knew as the rain cried down the roof

there would be no body for the elegy.

She died but it's only in the back Wards

we don't need to bother the newsman

from his busy day of kidnappings and serial killers

No one sees into our world, no galas are thrown,

our causes never drown in the bottom of one's wineglass.

We write our own elegies.

Hysteria

Hysteria:

this feminine word

this congenitally female term

the ancients conferred upon us

in their science and thought and form

we wild women, we hysterical ones

too much for men to contain

our mothers and grandmothers

locked away to set them free.

Hysteria is a woman's lot

uncontrollable

unbridled

wanton and tart

humanity and insanity conceived

in the dark night of the womb

those ancients knew the gate to birth

opens and lunacy escapes

two for a penny, one for a show.

Hysteria is a female name

my gender, a chimera

of mother-saint and whore

that vexing place of conception

revered and feared, obsessed of and cursed.

Chain us if you will, we soar inside

unbound by the fetters of sanity

undefiled by diagnosis or stain

citizens in this country of she-beasts

Hysteria, our motherland.

Learning the Galilean Moons

Father Galilei, looking out upon blanched

faces in the night sky

you gave Jupiter his dominion

and named those first moon-kingdoms.

So small and alabaster,

crude through your lens.

Could you imagine someday

I would stand in these halls watching the same sky,

forsaken as your Callisto?

How solemn are the halls tonight!

A line of children at the wall

awaiting their cures and potions

in paper cups ladled out from a window

in this timeless republic of lost stars

who wail and mourn in the night.

The rings of dust lay careless,

settled in our dozy minds

still shiny through a fitting lens.

We have held the book of Self and Ipseity

and signed our names softly in blood and snow within its pages

to receive the stain of diagnosis.

Our lives, our minutes inscribing the manuscripts
of cutting-floor films not meant to be seen Outside.
Someone sings a lullaby of cigarette curls and after-shock tears,
our brightness is ever dimming.
Like giants the sky whose death-cries we see
We will vanish long before anyone notices.

Beneath a vision of saints and apertures
the satin robe of time slips over, unawares
of the world Outside of men and country-
we wait for our turn in the showers,
collecting mementos in blue bowls and contraband cupboards
past, the halcyon hour of whispers
behind a head nurse's taut gaze.
We are beyond era;
our orbits severed from ordinary time.

They call us lunatics, but he calls cherubs,
flying with half-mended wings to our lessons
down these empty halls
to learn the hieroglyphics of a mind unsorted,
and all the wondering things of nature and sky.
The locks, a strange fixture on every door and window
of this cobbled-together school of nonsense
keeping us safe from all but each other.
Callisto, I know you too are lonely.

Father Galilei, looking out with your crude lens

You never saw my future face wavering in the distance!

But could it be,

when we have left these halls of illusion

when our tears have printed gem-tones in the tiles

will our shadows coat the walls in amber

will our madness streak the sky

where we stood at the windows in wonderment

learning the Galilean Moons?

Education

Once I was a writer.
I penned striking sentences
grammatically stunning in their fashion
lighting the countenance of any who chanced upon them.
But it has come to my attention
that my command of the language is slowly eclipsing.
Ebbing off into the night-air as seafoam dissipates on water.

Whose thought are these that crawl inside?
What thief has made off with *my* mind?

Perhaps it is the many hours of staring from the windows
cutting construction paper hearts
gluing glitter on cards to my inner child
and fighting over finger paints
or making magazine collages to earn
an hour of air inside the walls,
A cigarette snuck in the halls.

These side effects of sanity,
the making of one's lucid self
a clear mind, clean and empty
my marbles found and counted

Thank you!

Humility is a good medicine!

Hard to swallow, but pleasing to society.

I was once a writer- did I say?

I penned striking sentences

which made me believe I was *someone.*

But in captivity, one learns many things.

It has come to my attention

that my command of the language means nothing

if no one is listening to hear it

or that I am dead to speak it.

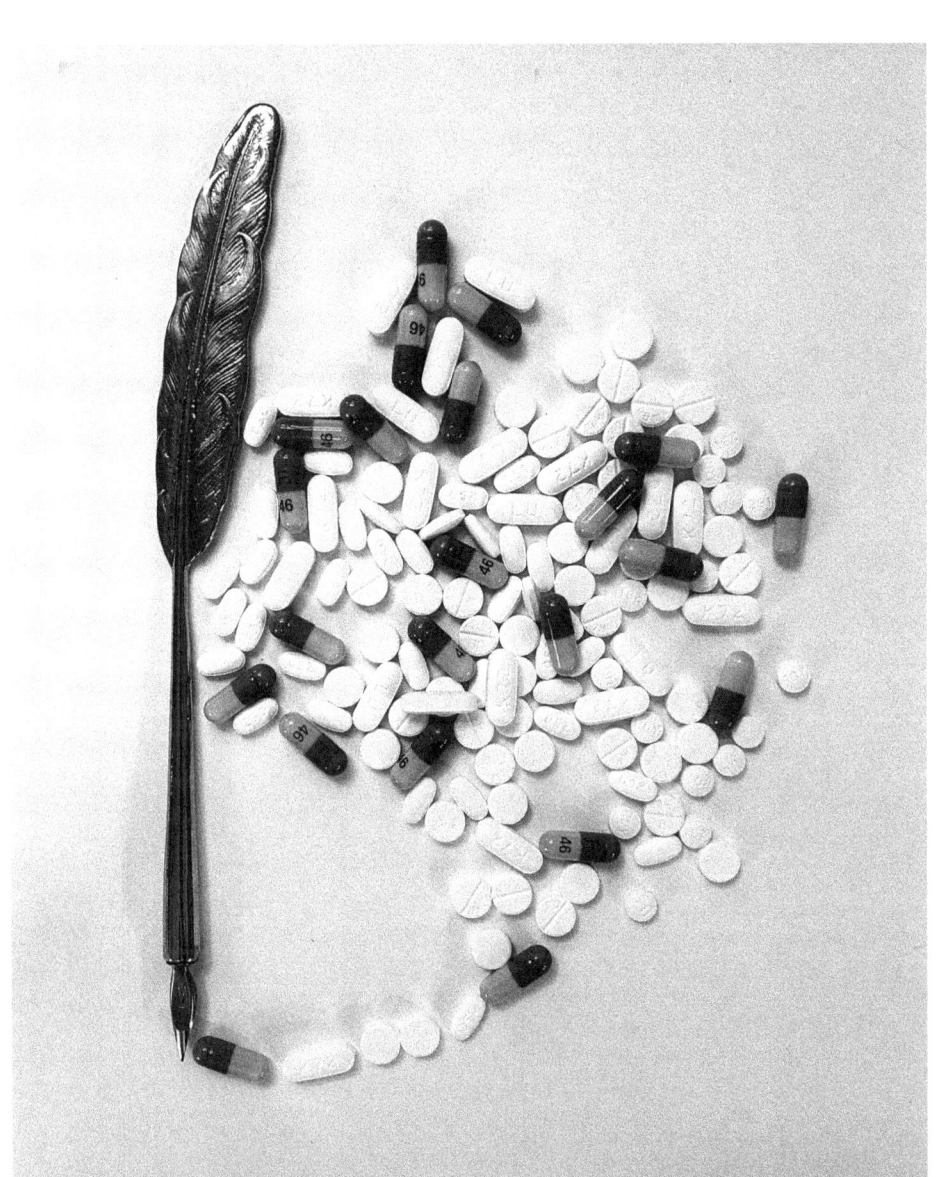

Legally Addicted

Authentic lunacy requires pills.

Straight jackets and chains shall no longer do.

This is modern madness,

bottoms up!

Take too few, you're unable to live.

Take too many and you're dead.

Pills in the morning

Pills in the evening

Pills in twilight, numbered like stars.

Rattle the bottles, Pavlov, here we come

for we'll never sleep again

once the jangling stops.

They cut a ray through the nightfall of depression,

they blur the blazes of manias.

They make us eat; they make us abstain,

they make us docile little monsters

putting silver bits in our bestial mouths to steer us

away from the avenues of ourselves.

Give us your poison so we can

age in the night, lost in the deserts of our mouths.

Swallowed in balloon-flesh,

our lovers left to wonder

if that headache will split us in two

should we turn away in the sheets once more?

We sacrifice our colour to the white, barren land

Of this sanity, this dope-sickness

the acceptable mood of sterility

where words suffocate under the

heaviness of chemical coercion

so murderers may never escape from within us.

Pills to sleep

Pills to wake

Pills to keep the horns from growing.

Hands shaking, face twitching

it must be working, I can't feel my feet

my head has rolled away.

And when the pills stop working

just electrocute my brain.

For stability has demands its price

for silencing the psyche

for deadening one's nature.

We sleep in front of the toilet

we wave goodbye to autonomy.

But it's all right, don't worry

We're legally addicted.

Transitioning

Then without prelude
the doors open,
I'm booted out
into a world not made for me.
I step around this hole I've dug,
this hole never to be filled again.
Though I shout, "I live!"
they turn away, deafened to me.
It's true, I died, I leave myself behind
in the white halls
strapped to an empty bed.
Part of me can never escape,
my roots have burrowed down in this world assigned to me.
A fraction of me runs out and stumbles
on the pavement, no-one takes heed.
So, I rise again, ready to put on a mask
to pretend it's all right
to pretend I *can* pretend
to try and live invisibly mad in plain sight
to put myself away in a box under the bed
to slide back in amongst Them
silent
hidden

a *real* girl

made of wood and paint and fluff.

The Secrets of Trees

All families have their secrets
all their trees, their deadened limbs
their roots, curled and hidden from sunlight
like uncles we never mention
whose names are concealed in leaf-veins
whose lives are buried down in hollows.
And even when AIDS comes culling
the crown knows not that its limb has fallen.

Imagine my surprise
to discover my name tucked behind the catkins.
My story, sewn into boughs weeping,
my insanity, a gall banished to the shade
to keep the trunk's strong appearance.
The crown knows not if I fruit or I die.
And it is its own oddity to me
that I find myself the *other* family secret.

The Therapists

Just who are these strangers we
invite in to scrutinize our hearts?
who are these foreigners
we bleed and die before?
How do they claim the right to ask
this impertinent entitlement to know?
How can they come at the beck of sawbones
and go at the whims of guarantors?
How do we pay these outlanders to care
but meter our trust out in drops?
And why do we refuse to say hello
only to decline to say goodbye?

What happens in the Silence?

What happens in the silence
when you and I both gaze?
Is this when the stars sing
their birth-names across the sky
and hope that we are listening
this very moment, you and I?

What happens in the silence
as you watch me dance about?
Is this when the spirits eavesdrop
and watch us like a show
cheering for their favourite characters
in a script that we don't know?

What happens in the silence
when you and I both smile?
Do lips meet in the afternoon
then secretly depart
to report our fleeting moments
on some great celestial chart?

What happens in the silence
when you and I both meet?

Do angels bring us nearer

when the words just cannot flow

revealing things I cannot tell

so you can finally, truly know?

Thursdays are Rain-Days

Thursdays are rain-days.
Drops of mercury hallow the window
in this time I share with you.
This room, with its shrines and statues of your
character peeking through
also conceals little silver boxes of my smiles and sighs
and nimble bits of my heart
for this is not your room, but mine
filled with my sounds, and words and world.

You fall and rise in my sight
and I, surely in yours.
A thousand and ten disappointments befall me like blue shards
as I realize your imperfections
as I realize how small and ugly you must see me
sprawled out and ornery before you.
Forgive me,
my intentions had not always been noble
and I spoke many times with unearned contempt.

Thursday-teacher,
we have long kept our scores

marked in stone strokes on gossamer tablets

tucked away under the chairs.

Flippancy is my mother-tongue

but avoiding, renders the harshest lessons

and though I may concede a secret

exchanged for a drop of your praise,

the margin comes ever closer; clumsy am I.

Thursday-mercury falls into our laps in tiny etched figures.

You have become cold these days.

I turn away from the windowpane, away

from my masquerade reflection.

The time is becoming thin, but you will not tell me thus.

So do not take these little words now as insolence,

but rather, instructions of love:

for we are almost done, and by the lesson of

one's student is a teacher taught.

Thursdays are Rain-Days: II

Seek a miracle in the twilight,
find a gift of light in the dim
But do not be remiss!
Lift up your head and close your eyes
for triumph comes in tiny whispers,
tinkling like secret, sparkling glass.

Come to the edge and shed your vassals
into the morning colour, cast your soul's true eyes.
I tell you, when one has very little
every grain becomes a treasure
its value measured in gratitude,
its worth beyond compare.

Do not be deceived by those who
would promise you a beautiful life
and speak of a painless way obtained
without suffering.
Is there a morning without twilight?
Is there a beginning not derived from an end?

Suffering is like a fire to temper the soul

and we all must learn to walk through fire,

for the stars are made of it

and offer their lives in a brilliance of it

and if we cannot walk through fire

we can never live amongst the stars.

Counsellor, it is fitting that we would part on a Thursday

Here then I would give to you the truth which my heart has bled to win:

that there must be evil in this world

for good to ascend to glory

and if failure never touched the earth

Victory should not belong to the mad ones.

Breakfasting in Shades of Insanity

The cups are laid out carefully
the kettle calls to come-
eggs and fruit and rashers
treacle, beans and toast.
Folding napkins, passing spoons,
you slice your pudding thinly,
you cut your eggs in fours.
Genteel, composed, and *humdrum,*
a template of mundane.

Across you I sit, entranced
by this quiet companionship.
The dead take their place beside me,
voices rustling in my ears.
The table candle's flame glows
smiling, laughing, yawning a demon's mouth,
consuming.
The sugar cubes are crying, gritty bits into my cup
in this play you cannot see.

You spread the paper in your lap
splashed with milk and the day's new murders.
Another death en masse, revealed

and you confide in me, *those lunatics always lurk behind such things.*

Those most American of things,

as if crazy were contained by geography.

This revelation between just you and I, shared:

spreading my bread with treacle,

I smile into a bite, hiding in plain sight.

We push our chairs back steadily,

place our forks and knives with care

and you crisply fold your paper

pushing away death for another day.

But the stain of association seeps into me, *profound*

as if the mad were synchronous, conjoined

like infinite sets of twins.

You draw back from malevolence, preserved

I am caught, fused in unwanted alliance.

We stand to make our goodbyes,

politely shake farewell.

And you pause, unsure of what you are seeing-

if some sort of familiar evil dwells here?

But you have never seen my mania for justice

nor my craziness for peace.

My lunacy for love escapes you,

this senility of never-ending hope, cannot be cut out of me.

So, I hide within your own blind eyes

trapped within that Manichean view

too compressed on this plane to breathe in colour,

no room at this table for shades of insanity.

A Synchrony in Flesh

We were expecting stained sheets,
you were seeking empyrean dreams.
But mine are of another sort:
a yearning sore of liberty.

For I have nothing left to offer,
I have nothing left to give.
I wore the scarlet dress *for you*.
But standing on the carpet to undrape
you must see
there is nothing left to show.
My bones, so very brittle now,
waiting for me to weep with remorse
stand like tiny spikes in defense against
your sudden, tentative rhythm.
My arms, slack and olden
quiver under white, waxed-paper skin
and cannot hold onto your neck.
There is no affection left in them, no strength.
For I may be granted parole for good conduct,
but I'm trapped in this cell for life.
And these breasts you once stroked and grazed on
have dissolved under white picket ribs,

curved in the grimace of Want.

You miss them, though.
You spill out words like *ghostly*
and *too thin*
and *fragile*.
But this *is* what you wanted, a synchrony in flesh.
Regardless, I am always "good enough."

For though you beg to differ,
though you'll say that I am beautiful
and you'll appeal your impartiality,
I see your eyes look elsewhere.
Know the axiom you demand in fantasies.
feel the groans you can't hear yourself make.
My worth, a recipe of numbers,
bedamned of a figure assigned.
You take according to your birthright,
and I give, cursed by mine.

I hear the implications, see the accusations
live the ramifications of your own
unctuous nervosa.

So then where is our answer?
Where is my escape but naught?

What weekly will wrap up this life in a quarter page

for younger women to note and avoid?

Then turn out this light now and see what you wish.

Fill me with your seed and leave me.

For I am tragically, beautifully useless.

That Curse to Stay and Live

Golden then, that afternoon, and brindled was the sky
fairytales still had an end,
and trains yet passed me by.
The news struck me between the eyes,
a cold, crushing crash within.
And dark the clouds did rust away,
the stars' shine snuffed to spoil.

The note you left behind,
when the wolf came to the door,
composed so thoughtfully like you,
asked for nothing more.
This life just could not hold you,
your soul, could not contain.
Your passions blazed too bright to own,
The curse of our kind come to claim.

The paper weaves an awkward tale:
an end, an unknown, a *sudden departure.*
As if the train had pulled out too early
without signs it meant to go.
We speak your tale, but eyes turn away to *easier* despair.
The whispers dance over the floor in vapors:

HowcouldheWhydidntheWhatwashethinking?

But I am cursed to know.

For there is no distance of mystery,

no wall of questions behind to hide.

The wolf is always at my door,

the howling, in my blood.

The glint of its eyes shines through the cracks;

its jaws, ready to dash my bones.

Now the mightiest of us has fallen,

what chance for *the rest* does yet lie?

We're a sorry caste of mourners, an inherited tribe of kin.

We've cobbled together this family,

we dance together through this ceremony of terms.

Orphaned by blood,

our DNA threads thick with grief.

A regalia of *rue*

that you clothed us in most tenderly,

when you accompanied that hound.

I do not ask your reasons,

but only how you left.

Why did it come to you that day?

Did it drag you with its claws?

And did you chase its tail and trace its steps?

Or in the last vestiges of your mourning, did you

see through its eyes over the edge of life

that bleeds into forever?

I must make myself remember

you are gone, *you dwell not here;*

and tie myself to the bed, the chair,

that I should not follow you *there*.

For I hear the howling call me,

I hear the baying, clear

I must cull away this sentiment,

I must snuff away this flame.

And take my curse with grace;

that curse to stay and *live*.

Hope, Get Back From Me

Get back, O Hope, and leave me,
take thy tattered vestiges and go.
We've danced our last sharp minuet.
This time,
our farewell burns ever closer.

Hope is the plaything of gods:
a curse to lead men blind to elysian
where spirits mean not them to go.
Hope is a noose and a knife to the back,
garroting us in the midst of our dreams.
Crushing beneath its weight,
it threads through with none opioid
ripping and pulling through fragile shards of vagaries.
Unraveling a stalwart desire,
blanching the colour of aspiration,
throwing it back to Apathy.

Hope makes her bed with Mourning.
Her sisters, Passion and Grace,
and Loss, her child, clings fast to her.
Her price, ten thousand tears
and her worth, ten thousand more.

Her requirement, the sacrifice of Want,

a penance of yearning demands.

Don't damn me then with such a light,

that throbbing pain of desire.

No ribbons of promise to strangle me in my sleep,

no faith to choke my soul.

Get back, O Hope, and leave me,

take thy tattered vestiges and go.

We've danced our last sharp minuet

This time,

our farewell burns ever closer.

The Ephemera of Mania

I have dropped the veils of fire
the tongues of light have leapt from my mouth.
I dreamed of lunar torches,
landscapes beholden only to the caravans of mythic gods
and now mine eyes have shaded from the siren beauties of Mania.
Even the hours become mercurial.
Now a dangerous dream I allow myself to wonder...
even as breath escapes me under a slow-falling mantel of despair,
I still find the strength to dream of blood and tears.

How fragile, how blue-petalled my limbs have become.
My spirit, it wears the rags of frost!
Gentleness has left the world,
even the stars have left my sight!
Has desperation hollowed me?
Have I learned death's embrace?
For I have become the suffering one
of Want, that sickness sore
and Melancholy, I don like silk.

Precarious, this walking between the poles
on crumbling turrets down paths of disconnected pearls

yet I know even *this* time is borrowed still.

The veils of fire ascend within my field once more

and memory is short, a lone mind is weak to refuse.

I shall take a sliver of moon

and carve upon my breast

a memento of despair, a memory of ecstasy

that in my element I would remember, yes

I would remember that I am an ephemeral one, cursed:

my steps must walk through fire, my soul must trod through sorrow.

What Nobody Tells You About Marrying a Mad Woman

We share a ring,

we share a bed

but we also share the dark things,

things obscured, you cannot ~~will not~~ see.

You see me as a woman:

a singular, a *one*.

But there are four of us *in situ*

divers, adhered, parallel.

Depression mania anorexia

These words are dull to you, flat on a page

but within:

a wolf, rabid

a unicorn, wanton

a child, starving.

They cling to me like leeches

that can never be detached.

Can you make love to all of us?

Can you hold us into age?

When you ask me to marry you,

who are you asking to stay?

For there are times when I will sacrifice to the wolf my willing flesh and times I will ride this unicorn into illusion

and times, that child placate above all else.

Is this bed big enough to shelter us?

Is this table ample to provide?

When I'm wrapped in yards of white,

they hide beneath my skirts.

And when I say these vows

they repeat, silently

vowing their fidelity to you, by dint of me.

They sit and wait and watch:

every row within these rooms

every kiss inside the doors

every act under secret sheets.

You'll tell me I am beautiful,

they won't let me see it.

You'll tell me I am cherished,

they won't let me feel it.

You'll promise me forever,

they won't let me hear it.

You'll wonder why you chained yourself

to a household full of cracks.

Yet, what nobody will tell you,

nobody will say:

Is that a mad woman will espy you,

she will see through your every guise.

She fears no demons you may bring with you,

flees no secrets you've withheld.

And she loves with wild abandon,

employs her madness as your shield.

So, if Darkness should ever take you,

I will find you

for my feet know the map of Sorrow well.

And if Grief should ever smother you,

I will slay it

for my hands have fought it ere and over .

If Life ever taketh what it gives,

I will sacrifice

for Denial's method is imprinted on my heart.

And if Love should ever leave you,

I will fill that hole

even t'were it torn into you by me.

All The Tears You Never See

The quiver of my lip, you call a *weakness*.

The shine in my eyes, *dramatic*.

But all the tears you never see,

running rivers between the hills of my breasts

disappearing in the sheets and pillows

evaporating around us

to grow harebells in the sink with dishwater.

All those tears you've never seen

tributaries of desolation,

solvent in the shower

serous in the rain.

Baptizing my feet in the name of Melancholy

this religion of despondency,

this sacrifice of self.

The weeping you can never see

imbued in strands of hair on the floor

running into my veins to bleed sorrow,

to hemorrhage salty despair.

You see the dam overflowing with regret

and it is *too much* for you

for you would drown in these seas

of the tears you never see.

Stigma

In this odd country of childhood
where no one ever grows old
or flies out free from the windows
because they're all boarded up,
my mind has become runny and diffuse
my limbs, incongruous beneath my skin.

You didn't see anything
you never heard the words
no one will believe you anyway-
no one trusts a crazy person.
And whatever you do, don't dare try to run
we'll catch you and eat you and no one will miss you.

But when I am set down to run back into the wild
like a caged creature given mercy,
I come down that hill with no triumph
as Moses, finding himself a stranger to a people left behind.
Experience is carved into my back,
a heart shattered and put back together with sand.

You'll pretend I did not exist for that time.
If I speak of this place, you will not listen,

if you ask of this place, I will not tell.

This system of checks and balances

muzzles us

and makes us all insane.

It's not enough to pad influential coffers

or to ink your ballots and shake your fists.

It's not enough to send your living dead off to

be buried alive out of sight

because you render us invisible,

because your discomfiture is killing us.

Do not your face away,

and be careful of the walls you build

with the heavy shame of your silence

lest you find your sons and your daughters

hanging over them,

these casualties of stigma.

Re-admissions

Back up the hill to the castle I flee

my carriage's red lights wailing:

Make way, the princess is come!

For she tried her luck out in this world

and found out like those before her

that sanity dances on the horizon

shimmering close like asphalt on a hot summer's day.

And when we reach out to grab it,

we find our hands seared

slapped back into our own mercurial kingdom.

The bandages they sent me out in have crumbled

Nothing holds me together.

But look, they've saved my bed for me

where these plastic-paper bracelets

are my only family jewels

and the crown I wear shines at 450 volts.

Welcome back, 5824

surely you know psychiatry is temporary

eventually you must all return,

for We'll save your life, but We won't teach you how to live.

I am draped in a robe stitched from blankets

I am carried on a litter of gurneys

I am locked up in a tower of dusk.

They will patch me up and send me back out to play

They'll carve out slivers and shards of me:

a snip under the clothing, a tuck inside a fold.

And when I return Outside, they'll see

my button-eyes dulled, my seams slapdashed together.

But where nobody sees in the secret places,

embroidered the account of how much I lost to gain.

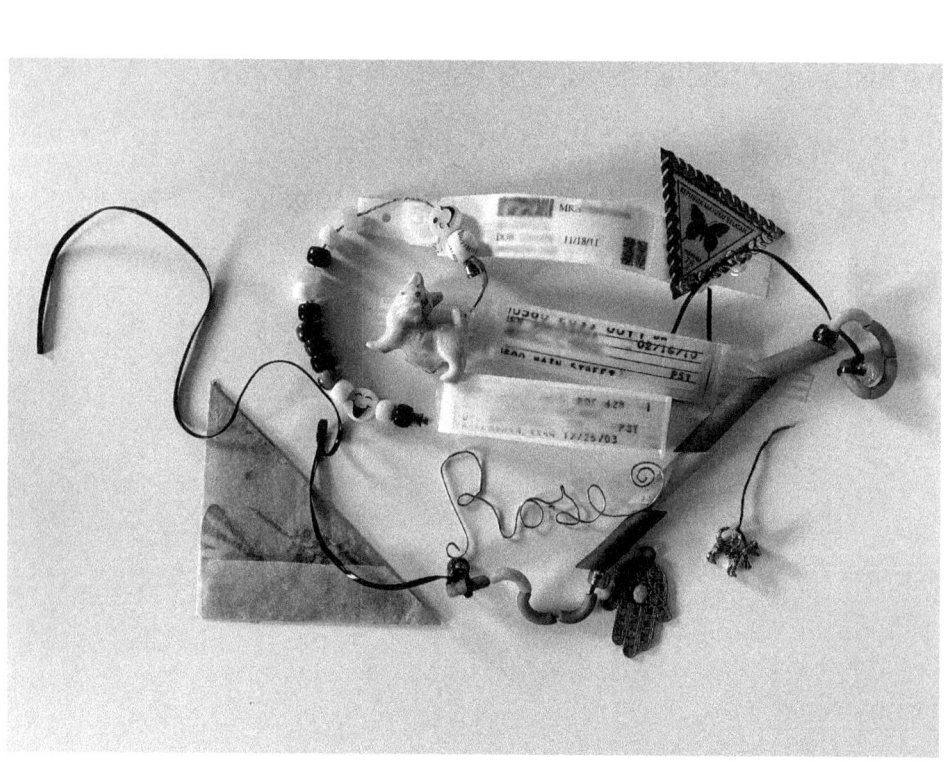

The House of Memorie

Once I had a memorie:
A house of a thousand windows,
with gingerbread trim and silvered panes.
The lanai filled with lavender;
a gazebo built of smiles.
Its roof was tiled in innocence,
its foundation of tender adages.
And all through this house passed
the light of grief:
a dwelling-place of dolor.

But storms came and assailed it.
Waves crashed through its stain-glassed door,
shattering every window
dashing the bricks to bits
seeping through its foundation
rearranging roof tiles.
Strangers came thundering through the lanai
scattering the gardens to splinters.

A shell remains, a silent husk
a pallid frame still stands.
Its windows shuffled aimlessly,

its panes shattered into mosaics, confounding.

Haphazardly are the tiles re-laid,

sediments fill the lanai.

The gazebo turns to a severed refrain.

No foundation endures

in this anachronism of dwelling.

This house, is called *amnesia,*

and all my memories within

have misplaced their chronology.

The map to which they were designed

taped back together hastily,

where yesterday was a year ago

and today has yet to be.

My story has crumbled, my authorship revoked;

my house, abandoned and foreclosed.

Red Doesn't Taste Good Any More

Overlooking the apex of Today and Tomorrow,

I sidestepped my written future

allowing Them to do to me as They would

allowing myself to sizzle

to crackle, to pop

to meld with lightning,

Transforming into liquid confusion

transposing this new girl

over the one who laid down meekly on this table

waking, *shocked*, as this stranger

speaking with an intruder's tongue

choking on spittle unfamiliar

trapped in this invader's frame

left in a foreign land with no signposts

to return with.

They wake me and ask me who I think myself to be.

When I don't know, they tell me:

Brain damaged

It's as good a name as any,

just tattoo it on my neck.

A nice man sits beside me

to feed me crumbs of my own story.

But I don't like this girl in his pictures

in his memories.

Soon he will leave me

soon he will go

soon I will stumble along in the hidden country

of a mind re-arranged,

disintegrating in plain sight.

I see faces in watercolour

laughing at my own foolish accord.

I am walking the labyrinth of thought,

never to trod again, my feet sliced off.

This map is full of holes.

All certainties fly away,

a thousand balloons drifting

a jungle gym of terms, unrecognizable:

cup, bell and *radiator*

Scents creep into my eyes

colours seep out of my ears

my skin understands, my mouth hears.

The geometry of things, edges softened like pudding.

I am a flattened country,

borders dissolved, disillusioned.

I drift, an unwelcome guest in this shell of a dwelling

and, rifling through the pages of a half-remembered tale,

a ghostly cheek presses, passing to mine

begging,

Recollect me, I am you, 5824!

Red doesn't taste good anymore.

Hallowe'en

Your screams still etch the floor tiles
loneliness peels from the walls
yellow corridors are full of your silent steps
the windows imprinted yet with your tears.
The echo of despair rings in the doorways,
the patterns of apathy cut forever in the ceilings.
Mania and psychosis still waltz in deserted courtyards
and your bones lay, unmarked, in these hallowed grounds.

As we mourn those who passed in these asylums
as their neglect still flows through our veins
we are bound by an illness that reaches from collective ancestry
beyond demographics of identity.
But on this day of merriment
They trod through these temples of memoria
without thought of the actuality of our past.
They are not schooled in terror, and so
have the foolish love of fear
because they know it will have its end for them.

After their videos are filmed and uploaded,
after they've screamed and laughed and boasted

of their bravery amongst ghosts and spirits,

after they've gone home from these asylums

and told these illusory tales for another year,

we will return to honour our dead

at our altars of the omitted

to lift up the unnamed, the erased,

the abused and downtrodden and experimented-on

For as all ancestors must,

they went the way before us

paving the road in stones of their suffering

making the way wide to some future freedom

leading us into this era *Outside*

imperfect, but ever-widening

these streets escaping Bedlam.

Hallowe'en

for Them the day of guise, of revelry

for us, the day of Remembrance.

This Has Always Been Our Country

It was the day the world closed:
hung out its sign, sent everyone home
drew its blinds and closed its eyes
to tremulous sleep, indefinitely.

Its children forgotten, they minded their own
and passed over that threshold
as if through a looking-glass
into a land identical;
indiscernible from their own.
Into a land uncertain,
a world long-occupied by lunatics
conditioned by institutions,
where thoughts must slow and stagger
where time clots like syrup
where the wariness of contamination
conducts its constant separation between them.
Where the mind must be kept busy
lest one's intellect run down one's chin
where one is paralyzed at the doorstep by what may happen next
and that despair of being, cementing ones' shoes
under waters of lament.
An uncertain world where people stay distant,

where something's always out to kill you

but this danger, one cannot see.

It was the year the world closed.

and these novices, these newlings

fell heavy against the door

tumbling headlong into insanity.

Don't fear, we're here to *catch* you

to walk beside you and behind you

before you and below you.

You've come into *our country*, we have always been here watching.

I open the door to usher you in,

all past transgressions forgotten.

For we are peoples of dignity,

and though you look at us as *violent*

I look back at you with *grace*.

I will not leave *you* behind in exile,

I will not banish *you* from this gate.

So welcome to our world,

come, reach out and take my hand.

I'll take you through our process,

this business of becoming mad.

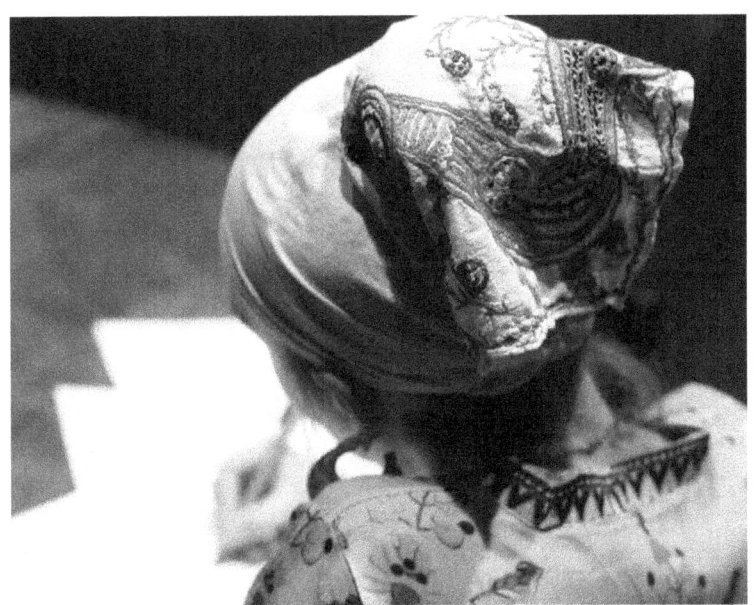

K. Rose Quayle is a New Orleans native who resides in Pittsburgh, PA. She is the author/illustrator of *Look Left, Walk Green: A Shocking Tale of Losing the Past and Choosing to Gain the Future*, *The Book of Moon*, and *Skittle's Little Book of Kitten Wisdom*. Her writings focus on the first-hand experience of living with a mental illness in order to educate and reduce mental health stigma.

www.ingramcontent.com/pod-product-compliance
Lightning Source LLC
Chambersburg PA
CBHW051158290426
44109CB00022B/2500